Timeless Venice

by Mark Robinson
designed by Hilary Sadler

PALLAS ATHENE

Contents

	page
About this CD-ROM	1
The map	5
Jacopo de' Barbari	19
The achievement of Jacopo and his colleagues	27
Epilogue	43
Author's note	47
Some Italian and Venetian terms	50
Locations of original prints	51
Main sources consulted	52
How to buy prints of the map	55
Trouble-shooting	56

Note: References in this text shown thus: *(INDEX/Fontego dei Tedeschi)* indicate a reference in the CD-ROM which can be found by clicking the mouse button on the words shown. In this case, click on the yellow INDEX button when it appears on the screen. When the index page follows, click on the line 'Fontego dei Tedeschi'.

Illustrations in this booklet are from the restored version of Jacopo de' Barbari's map of Venice in 1500, by kind permission of the publishers and copyright owners, Edizioni Tedeschi Marco (see 'How to buy prints of the map').

About this CD-ROM

TAKE A UNIQUE TOUR of the loveliest city in the world. Explore canals, squares and alleys… visit nearby islands… see world-famous hotels and churches as they are today … all in a huge map printed 500 years ago!

Only one map, one city in the world, lets you do this. The city is Venice. The map is Jacopo de' Barbari's giant drawing of the city in 1500. Jacopo shows his city in incredible detail – not only canals, bridges and buildings, but doors, windows, and chimney-pots. And Venice has changed so little, even after five centuries, that his map still remains a reliable guide to much of the city.

Now, for the first time, the magic of the computer brings this great masterpiece into your home, with side-by-side colour photographs showing what has changed, and what is still the same.

'Timeless Venice'

The new CD-ROM 'Timeless Venice' is a must for lovers of Venice and of history. Following Jacopo's map through the city, it...

- ❖ Introduces a selection of outstanding points in the map, with side-by-side photos and spoken commentary (about 5 minutes)

- ❖ Zooms in on topical details: the clock tower, brand new in 1500; men working in the Arsenale; a platform ready for a public execution; the original Regata, oldest regular sporting fixture in the world; and many others

- ❖ Takes you a walk from the civic centre to the modern city hospital, comparing old and new along the way, with commentary (about 7 minutes)

- ❖ Explores points of interest chosen by you, with a brief commentary on each one – 145 visits and a total of over 90 minutes sound recording

❖ Shows details in 1500 side-by-side with recent colour pictures – more than 140 photos

❖ Lets you browse through the huge map in almost full size

❖ Offers a clear on-screen Index of points of interest. Just click – and your choice comes up on screen

❖ Is extremely easy to navigate, with a 'Home' button always available. You simply cannot get lost!

'Timeless Venice' is an exciting, informative experience. If you know Venice, it is a fascinating reminder. If you do not know it, you will certainly want to!

The following pages are about Jacopo de' Barbari and his great work. Further chapters offer interesting sidelights, including how to obtain your very own print of the map.

The map

IT IS SURELY a happy coincidence that the most detailed town map surviving from the early 16th century should depict the one great city whose major features have changed hardly at all in the last five hundred years. The city is Venice: the map is Jacopo de' Barbari's bird's-eye view, licensed for duty-free sale on October 30, 1500. Strictly speaking, it is a perspective drawing, not a map: but map is a short and convenient word, and I shall continue to use it here.

Jacopo's map is a huge woodcut measuring 2.82m wide by 1.35m high, or more than nine feet by four. The six wood blocks from which it was printed stand in the Correr Civic Museum in St Mark's Square, Venice. Two of the blocks have been slightly altered twice, once in about 1514, once later. There are about a dozen known prints from the first state in museums and collections in Europe and the United States, including the best preserved copy of all in the British Museum, London, and another dozen from later states.

Jacopo's map is unique. A few large views of cities are known to have been made earlier, including one of Rome measuring more than 1 by 2 metres, which exists now only in a painting copied from the original print. None of these known views begins to approach Jacopo's in the wealth or accuracy of its detail, and none can be said to represent the modern city. Yet with little more than a handful of exceptions, every canal, square and alley in Jacopo's map of Venice still exists, playing the same part as thoroughfare or marketplace in the life of the city as it did sixty years before the birth of Shakespeare.

With Jacopo as our guide, we can walk from the former cathedral of San Pietro in Castello in the north-east, past the once mighty Arsenal, to the little church of San Nicolo dei Mendicoli in the south-west, by the same routes that Carpaccio, Titian or the Bellinis might have taken. In this CD-ROM we can find our way from the city centre to the present-day hospital via the alleys and squares where they would have walked *(HOME/FIND)*. We can check our time by the same clock as we pass the same frontage of St Mark's: and with the shades of these great Venetians we can rejoice over many buildings still standing that were landmarks in their day, grieve for many that have vanished, and perhaps occasionally admire some that have taken their place.

The map was published by one Anton Kolb, described as a German merchant in the application which he made to the authorities for exemption from export duty. Thanks to eleven centuries of stable government (and

possibly to a dislike for throwing things away) Venice is the best documented city in the world, and a record of Kolb's application is still on file. In it he pleads that the map has taken more than three years to complete, not only because of the difficulty of making an accurate plan but also because of its size, which has required sheets of paper larger than any made before and has demanded the latest techniques of printing large formes. One wonders whether Kolb would have found modern bureaucrats as understanding as the Signoria: it granted him freedom from duty and protection against plagiarism for a period of four years. Kolb's is the only name mentioned in connection with the map in contemporary records. The identity of the artist was not stated, and was the subject of much speculation until the authorities finally agreed on Jacopo de' Barbari. The map itself contains an interesting sidelight on this identification. *(INDEX/Walch)*.

When we have looked a little further into the map and its making, we shall certainly find ourselves wondering what was its purpose. Why did Kolb and his colleagues go to so much trouble for what could not have been a particularly remunerative endeavour? The only suggestion I have seen in print is that the map would have been useful to foreign merchants visiting Venice who wanted to call on their business contacts. Without intending disrespect to authority, I must say that this seems inherently improbable. Every Venetian would have known in 1500, as he knows today, exactly where every important citizen could be found, and the visitor would have been whisked to his destination by boat within minutes. Moreover, we have only to watch for a moment the tourists wrestling with their Visceglia and Tabaco maps in a stiff breeze, to disembarrass ourselves of the idea that a nine-by-four-foot map would have made a handy guide for visitors.

However, we who have recently survived the celebration of a new millennium are at an advantage over earlier writers, and I believe that we can think of a more likely reason for the map's publication, namely that it was what we would call today a public relations exercise to greet a very special new year. True, the year 1500 marked only a half-millennium, but it did not pass unnoticed. There was a body of opinion that it heralded the end of the world: and we may assume that there were also at least some optimists who took a more cheerful view of it, and chose not to wait another 500 years for their celebrations.

Venice in 1500 was the most exciting city in the world, its image similar to that of London in the 1910s or New York in the 1950s, the place where everything was happening. It was already a thousand years since the original settlers had fled from the barbarian terror on the mainland to the mud banks of the lagoon, and seven hundred years since their descendants had founded the stable and capable government which, give or take an assassination or two, was to last until Napoleon destroyed it in 1797. Only two invaders had ever disturbed Venice's tranquil progress in the lagoon: Pepin's Frankish troops, who were cut to pieces on the treacherous mud flats in 809, and the ancient rival Genoa, which was finally defeated at Chioggia in 1380.

Thanks to its happy situation in the Adriatic Sea and to the bravery and commercial enterprise of its citizens, Venice had attained a near-monopoly of the important trade between Europe and the East across the Mediterranean, and a degree of prosperity far beyond any other city in Europe. While it was governed by an oligarchy of wealthy and long-established families, the ordinary man in the street was very conscious of his status as a Venetian. And though its citizens were subject, at least theoretically, to laws which placed rigorous limits on the display of personal wealth, the city itself was the greatest show on earth.

It is surely to be expected, then, that some clever entrepreneur would have conceived the idea of celebrating Venice at the moment of the half-millennium, a celebration which would not only show the glory of the city in visible terms but would do so by the use of the new technology that had swept the

THE MAP

world within living memory, and that flourished particularly in Venice – the amazing new art of printing. That clever entrepreneur was Anton Kolb, whose application to the Signoria goes some way towards reinforcing the public relations' theory, since he claims that the map has been made principally to enhance the fame of Venice. Kolb may also have seen his great project as a public relations exercise not only for the city, but in particular for himself and his fellow German merchants. *(INDEX/Fontego dei Tedeschi)*.

The price of the map was three ducats or florins. Comparison with present-day values is bound to be suspect, but Schulz tells us that five ducats a month was the salary of a top-ranking artist working at the Doge's Palace in 1500, and that a portrait commissioned from Alvise Vivarini in 1494 cost twelve and a half ducats. According to Pignatti, three ducats was the price of a luxurious robe, and de' Barbari paid 24 ducats in Nuremberg in 1500 for a horse.

A ducat contained slightly more than three grams of gold, so if we base its value on the gold prices prevailing at the beginning of 2002 when this note was written, the map cost very roughly 20 pounds sterling, 29 U.S. dollars or 33 euros. Pignatti tells us that about a hundred impressions could have been made from the wood blocks, and that prints were taken as long as three hundred years later. When one considers the amount of work that must have

gone into the map during the three years that it took to produce, a gross sales return of two thousand pounds over three centuries hardly seems excessive, and we may think it fortunate that the enterprising Kolb had other interests that provided him with a living.

What strikes one first is the astounding detail of the map. Drawn from an imaginary aerial viewpoint to the south-east of the city, it shows or purports to show every window in every building, and every tree in every garden, that would have been visible to an infinitely keen-eyed observer on a perfectly clear day in 1500.

Having a literal mind, and having seen a few earlier and later views of Venice which contained glaring omissions and inaccuracies, I began to wonder just how accurate Jacopo's view really was. So I noted the name and location of every *palazzo* and *casa* – that is, every private house – that I could find listed in Lorenzetti's *Venice and its Lagoon*, the greatest of all guide books to the city, as having been in existence in 1500. Where the postal number of a house was given, I wrote that down as well. This proved to be something of a hazard: the endearing eccentricity of the Venetian post office means that most house numbers in Venice are in the thousands, and owing to the appalling proof-reading in English of Lorenzetti's publishers, about one address in seven turned out to be wrong, usually through transposition of digits. I then trudged round the city with a camera and a compass, photographing every building on my list that could be photographed from the public highway and noting its orientation. I have since 'collected' several more houses that I have found in other books and one or two that I have found for myself.

In all, I photographed and noted well over a hundred pre-1500 houses. In the natural order of things, however, they face in every possible direction: and many, though their location could be seen clearly enough in Jacopo's map, did not present a clear enough face to the south-east to offer a worthwhile comparison with a present-day photograph. In the end I was left with thirty-odd houses, some of which are little altered superficially since 1500, while others are altered but retain quite major recognisable features. We shall come across these houses in our exploration of the map. Drawings of the *palazzi* shown in this CD-ROM range from about 7 by 9mm (¼ by ⅓ inch) to 27 by 36mm (1 by 1⅜ inches). With only a few exceptions, any of them could be obliterated by a small postage stamp. *(1-HOME/TOUR. 2-INDEX/Pal Benedetti.)*

First, however, to the map itself. Jacopo's map, as I have said, was printed from six wood blocks. The arrangement and approximate print

THE MAP

areas of the six sheets are shown below. The existing original copies were printed on six sheets, but later from time to time copies were printed on twelve or twenty-four sheets, perhaps for convenience in printing or handling, perhaps because of difficulties in obtaining such large sheets of paper. A third possibility is that Kolb's huge printing press, which must have been specially made for this job, was useless for anything else and was dismantled for scrap.

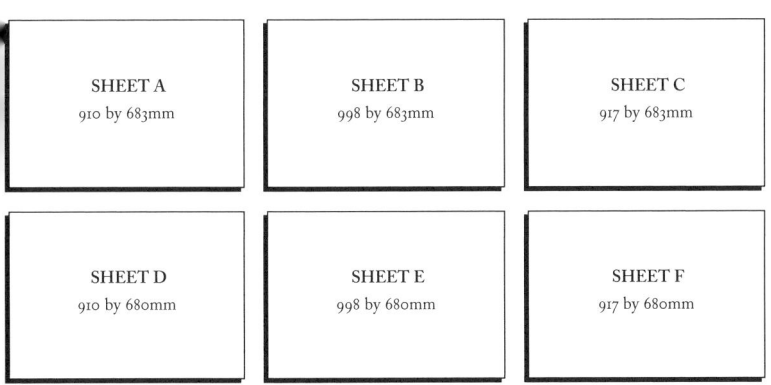

SHEET A
910 by 683mm

SHEET B
998 by 683mm

SHEET C
917 by 683mm

SHEET D
910 by 680mm

SHEET E
998 by 680mm

SHEET F
917 by 680mm

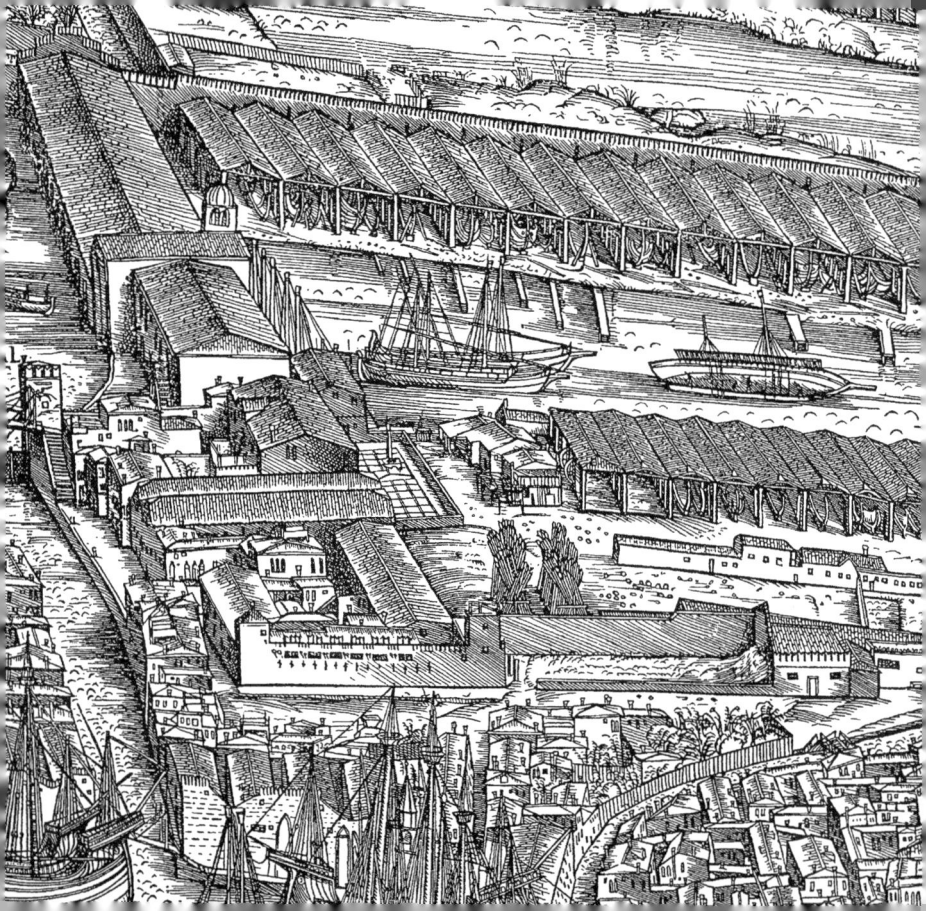

THE MAP

The blocks are made from pear wood, each consisting of vertical planks joined together. In the course of time, fissures have opened between planks which have resulted, in later prints, in vertical blank lines where the ink has not been applied. Over the years, various attempts have been made to reinforce the junctions between planks with horizontal strips of wood and metal butterfly joints. Recent restoration has aimed to increase the stability of the assembled blocks, and to protect them from damage by insects.

The blocks were last used in 1838 to print four copies of the map on the occasion of the visit to Venice of the Emperor of Austria, then the occupying power. It is not recorded what kind of press was used, but by that time the venerable blocks were long past their best, and may well have been damaged further by this printing.

Today they occupy a well-lit glass case in the Correr museum, side by side with a photocopy of the map. It is fascinating to see groups of Venetian schoolchildren sitting enthralled on the floor, while a knowledgeable and inspiring lecturer on the museum staff introduces them to this part of their heritage.

Jacopo de' Barbari

SHEET C of the map is disappointingly empty at first glance: yet it turns out to contain one of the map's most interesting features.

This is the gentleman with the beard, ringlets and battered nose who represents the *Grecale* or north-east wind (also called *Vulturnus*), because in this face Pignatti believes that he recognises the subject of a 17th-century portrait of one Jacob Walch by an engraver named Fennitzer in a series entitled *Painters of Nuremberg*. Jacob Walch of Nuremberg is known to have been one and the same person as Jacopo de' Barbari of Venice. *(INDEX/Walch)*

Details of Jacopo's life remain largely a mystery. The date of his birth is unknown, even within wide limits, and current estimates vary between 1446 and 1475. If the north-east wind is in fact a self-portrait, the earlier date would seem to be a better guess. His name offers another problem. Balistreri-Trincanato notes the suggestion, prompted by the typically Jewish ringlets in his Grecale sketch, that Jacopo might have been of proselytised German Jewish extraction, sponsored by the Barbaro family who may themselves have come originally from Germany.

It is likely that Jacopo went to Germany as a fairly young man. In 1490 the Emperor Maximilian despatched a message from Nuremberg to Buda by his 'musician Jacopo Barbiria'; Jacopo de' Barbari is known to have been in Maximilian's service ten years later, and also to have been a musician, so it is probable that he and 'Barbiria' are the same person.

Jacopo exercised an early influence over the younger Albrecht Dürer, who wrote in the preface to his *Theory of Proportions:* 'I find no one who has written on the rules of human proportions except a man named Jacopo, born at Venice and a delightful painter'. Dürer is known to have been impressed by drawings which Jacopo showed him of a male and female figure constructed according to certain anatomical rules: evidently Jacopo was a considerable theorist and this appealed to Dürer, who spent much of his life trying to harmonise artistic ideas of proportion, perspective and philosophy. It is likely that they first met in 1495.

In April 1500, by which time Jacopo's work on the map of Venice would have been completed and handed over to the engravers and printers, the Emperor Maximilian gave him a one-year contract as portraitist and miniaturist with a stipend of 100 florins, and in the same month a payment of 24 florins was recorded to Jacopo *'Wellische Maler'* to buy a horse. Later he was also referred to as *'Jacob der weylische Meister'*. The word *weylische* is obviously related to the Old English *waelisc* meaning 'foreign' from which are derived both the word Welsh and the surname Walsh. In precisely parallel fashion 'Jacob der weylische Meister', the 'foreign master', became Jacob Walch and under this name he found his way into German history books and into Fennitzer's engraving. Historians are certainly agreed that Walch and de' Barbari are the same person. In addition it seems to me that his German name takes the form of a gentle pun on his Venetian name.

Not all foreigners at Nuremberg were called Walch, after all, and I would suggest that *Walch* 'the foreigner' is not too bad a pun on *de' Barbari* 'of the barbarians'. (In a similar way Dürer's German name seems to derive from his father's origin in the Hungarian village of Ajtas, *ajto* in Hungarian and *dür* in German both meaning 'door'.)

Pignatti points out an interesting echo of Jacopo's German experience in the writing of *Vulturnus*, the name of the easterly scirocco, beneath his supposed self-portrait, in that it is spelt here with a capital F – the way that a German would pronounce it. We may notice the same thing in reverse in sheet B, where the caption to the church of S Sofia is spelt with a *v* instead of with an *f*.

Apart from his possible errand to Buda for the Emperor Maximilian in 1490, nothing definite is known about Jacopo before his employment by Maximilian in 1500. In 1504 a settlement of accounts is recorded between Maximilian, Jacopo and Anton Kolb for work done since 1500, which is important in that it confirms that Jacopo and Kolb were working together at least immediately after the publication of the map. The nature of this collaboration is not known, but it may have been concerned with a projected work on Germany with Jacopo as illustrator and Kolb as editor.

During 1503 Jacopo worked for the Grand Duke of Saxony at Wittenberg, where he met Dürer, and elsewhere. He met Dürer again at Nuremberg in 1504 and also perhaps on Dürer's visit to Venice in 1506. It was on this last occasion that Dürer wrote to his friend Pirckheimer of his discovery that there were better painters than Jacopo in Venice adding, perhaps just a little crossly: 'Anton Kolb still swears that there are none better'. Up to this point, however, Jacopo had evidently been a considerable influence on Dürer, and even this statement need not detract from Jacopo's authority as a draughtsman.

In 1507 and 1508 Jacopo was probably in Heidelberg and Brandenburg, where portraits by him are recorded. In 1509 he seems to have worked for Count

JACOPO DE' BARBARI

Philip of Burgundy, recently returned from his embassy in Rome, on the redecoration of his castle at Suytburg on the North Sea. Philip had been greatly taken with the new Renaissance styles in Italy, and Jacopo as a not-too-extreme Renaissance Italian may have made a particular appeal to him. Jacopo seems to have ended his life contentedly in the service of Philip's sister the Grand Duchess Margaret of Austria, regent of Holland. Several payments to him are recorded in 1511 including one to 'our well-beloved *valet de chambre* and painter Maitre Jacques de Barbary' which he has acknowledged with his signature and his emblem of the caduceus, and which was intended to help him pay for his lodgings, the doctor, a travelling trunk, a coat, and the making of his Will.

In the same year Margaret granted him a pension on account of his 'age and infirmity' (hardly likely if he was born in 1475, since he would then have been only 36): and in an inventory at Lille of her possessions in 1516 are listed works by 'the late Maitre Jacopo de Barbary'. An inventory of 1524 also mentions various works, portraits, miniatures and engravings by Jacopo which are dispersed with her estate. Dürer enters this story finally in 1521, when he asked Margaret if he might have Jacopo's sketch book: she replied that she had already promised it to the painter Bernhard van Orley, probably to use for paintings for her court.

Jacopo is therefore known historically as a successful and busy artist for at least ten years of his life, although fewer than a dozen of his paintings and thirty or so of his engravings are known to exist, and these the critics seem to agree are of no great distinction. To my inexpert eye, at any rate, they do not radiate the assurance and authority that inform every inch of the map of Venice, and it is little wonder that Jacopo for so long was overlooked as a candidate for its authorship. Only in the mid-1800s was he suggested as the probable author on grounds of style: and although by the end of the century all critics were agreed on this, it was not until the discovery of the Fennitzer engraving, which Pignatti believes must have been based on a lost self-portrait of Jacopo, that the evidence for his authorship could be called complete.

I dare not put my next thought as anything but the most speculative of questions: how many one-picture artists are there in history? In music one can think of many composers who produced a large volume of music in their lifetime but are known today mainly for one or two works: they include names like Bruch, Chaminade, Field, Hummel, Lalo, Litolff, Macdowell, Moszkowski, Rubinstein, Scharwenka. But music remains unheard until performers invest time and effort in playing it, whereas a graphic artist's work is there to be seen by all. It must be true that the element of fashion plays a

JACOPO DE' BARBARI

large part in determining an artist's success. Would Canaletto be so well known today if Venice had not been one of the obligatory stops on the well-to-do Englishman's Grand Tour? Or indeed if Venice had since become a concrete-and-glass jungle?

What puzzles me is this. Jacopo's map of Venice speaks for itself in every line as a supreme masterpiece: yet it was made by an artist who, on the known remainder of his work, cannot be described as more than thoroughly respectable. Was he in fact a genius of the bird's-eye view who only once was given the chance to prove himself? If the fashion had been for bird's-eye views of cities rather than for portraits and religious or mythological subjects, would Jacopo today be a world-famous master and Titian a comparatively obscure footnote in the history books? It is a tantalising thought.

The achievement of Jacopo and his colleagues

SOME PERSPECTIVE may be gained on the achievement which Jacopo's map represents if we think for a moment on the state of the world in the year 1500.

England's first Tudor monarch, Henry VII, had been on the throne a mere fifteen years. His son, the future Henry VIII, was a lad of nine. The mother of Queen Elizabeth I, Anne Boleyn, was not yet born. Martin Luther was twelve years old, John Calvin would not be born for another nine years. The foundation stone of St Peter's in Rome had not been laid. Copernicus, the first scientific revolutionary, was aged 27 but his great work would not be published until long after Jacopo's death, and Jacopo doubtless shared the common belief that the sun moved round the earth. Galileo, who demonstrated in Venice the telescope that would have been such a help to Jacopo, did not do so until a century later.

Men believed that everything was composed of earth, air, fire and water: illness was caused by humours in one or other part of the body: alchemists sought the secret that would transmute base metals into gold.

But although modern investigative science was non-existent, certain crafts were well developed. The most obvious is building: the cathedrals of Torcello, Chartres and Salisbury had been built by men who may not have been able to write their names, but who possessed empirical knowledge of a quality that has kept their work standing to this day. Weaving, woodworking, leathercraft and metalwork were well advanced. The twin arts of astronomy and navigation were developed in a practical way as far as they could be without improved instruments (for example, the telescope) and at least well enough to permit accurate navigation in the Mediterranean, the only sea that was then of much importance to people in Europe.

The state of the art of surveying, on which modern map-making depends, presents something of a puzzle. The roads and aqueducts built by the Romans make it clear that they were practical surveyors of a high order. Yet map-making of any quality simply did not exist. True, the duplication of accurate maps had had to await the advent of printing, since scribes could not be relied upon to copy maps with even tolerable accuracy: true also that the size and wealth of populations had not yet made it essential to define ownership of land within close limits in writing. But to our fact-ridden minds it still comes as a surprise to find that a civilisation that had worked out the geometry of planes and solids, and had produced the graphic skills of Leonardo, Dürer,

Carpaccio and the Bellinis, had not yet developed the ability (or perhaps the interest) to make accurate representations of the ground under its feet.

There is still considerable controversy about the methods used to produce Jacopo's map, and it is not for me to pronounce judgment. On the one hand it is argued that the map contains errors and distortions which indicate that it was a work of imagination rather than the result of a survey. On the other hand is the view that the art of surveying was sufficiently well advanced by 1500 for the map to have been created as the result of careful measurement of angles and distances, and that this is its most likely source.

Measuring distances presents special problems in Venice, with its acute shortage of straight lines, and I will only dare to point out that Jacopo may not have felt it necessary to measure distances: he could have made a perfect scale plan showing all the *campanili* in the city by measuring the angles between them, and then reproducing these angles on paper (assuming, of course, that the instruments used to measure and draw angles were sufficiently accurate). One would not know what the scale was, but Jacopo did not need to know this: he could have drawn a ground plan to any scale he wanted, and interpolated details from memory or from on-the-spot notes. Once given his ground plan, he could then have worked out his perspective from known principles.

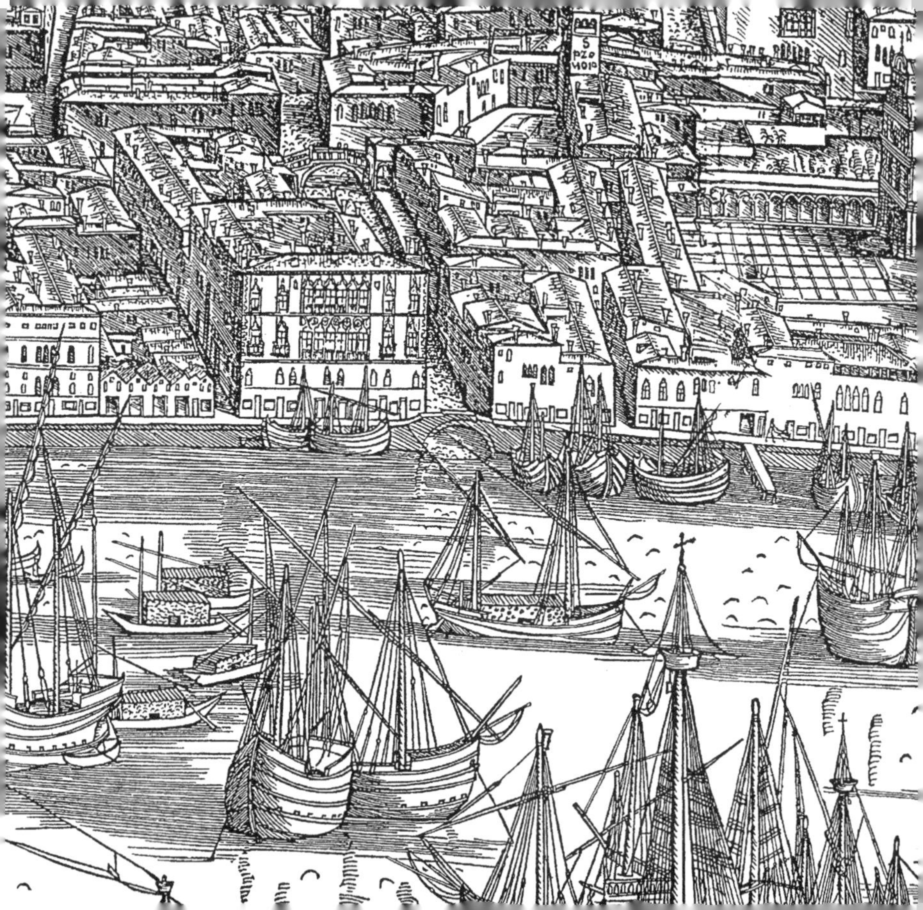

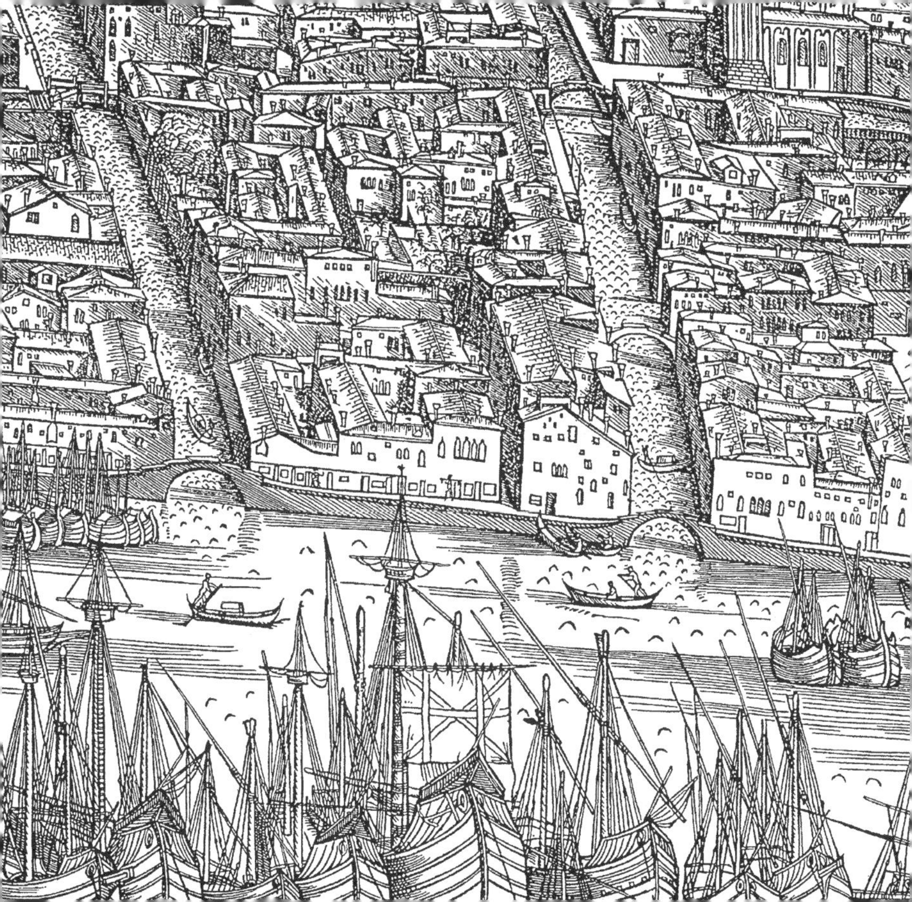

TIMELESS VENICE

It has been remarked that even allowing for the effect of perspective, the scale of the map diminishes from east to west, with the suggestion that this was somehow accidental. It is worth noting, however, that this adjustment of scale has enabled Jacopo to place the area round Piazza San Marco and the Doge's Palace, which are close to the physical centre of the city, decidedly to the left of centre in his map, allowing him to increase their apparent grandeur and also that of the Arsenale, which in 1500 was still of great military and political importance. This seems to accord well with Kolb's stated aim 'to enhance the fame of Venice'.

In any case, whatever the map's purpose, and whether or not it was based on a survey in the modern sense, we have to marvel at the astonishing wealth of detail in which it shows *palazzi* that are standing today. Jacopo could not have known that five centuries later, of all the buildings he depicts, these *palazzi* would still be there for us to photograph: so we have to accept that most major features he shows us bear the same relation to actuality as these do. This can only mean that he, alone or with a team of assistants, collected views of every building and open space in the city, with copious notes on its details, size and orientation, before the map could be made. Let us notice that his task included carefully worked-out placing of quarter-tones and half-tones to represent shadows, so that his map gives the impression of a view that is not only solid but instantaneous (though it has to be said that recent work casts some doubt on the veracity of this impression).

Following the practice of the time, Jacopo would then have transferred the design in reverse onto the huge wooden blocks, so that they would print the right way round. Not until each block was finished and accurately matched to its neighbours could the woodcutters go to work on the surface with their knives, gouges and chisels, till at last there stood in relief only the lines that Jacopo had drawn.

An almost miraculous technique is revealed in the way that he depicts the buildings and open spaces in his map as if from a single viewpoint, although no such viewpoint exists or ever existed in actuality. Even had there been an accurate survey of the canals and alleys on which the buildings were set, there remained the problem of obtaining adequate information about the appearance of each building or space in the city: and by any standards at any time this amount of information-gathering would be a daunting prospect. To a present-day photographer tramping round Venice in search of perhaps a hundred well-identified buildings, the idea of 'collecting' the several thousand buildings in the city without the help of Lorenzetti's guide or the post office list, and of recording sufficient detail of their appearance and dimensions, seems impossibly daunting. Today's photographer, moreover, will appreciate very clearly that the buildings of Venice do not all obligingly display themselves from a south-easterly viewpoint: some can be seen only from the canals, some only from land, and some are so closely crowded together that the normal camera lens cannot contain them.

But whatever the difficulties, the information was in fact collected in the closing years of the 15th century. One can only imagine the amount of paper that must have been thrown away, and grieve for the loss of such a treasury of contemporary detail. Then came the task of collating this mountain of information, of taking the details of each individual building or open space from its available viewpoint and with whatever dimensions and surface detail had been noted locally, and re-depicting it as if from the air.

We have become accustomed today to seeing 'computer graphics' on our television sets. A designer of, say, a new motor car has only to feed details of lines and dimensions into a computer and, lo, the computer can depict the car as it would be seen from front, back, left, right, top or bottom. This is in a real sense an electronic extension of the science of perspective, which itself was only a century old in 1500. (We may recall Leonardo's drawing of an artist using a grid of crossed threads to view a reclining model whom he is

ṡ. īo. batiſta.

S mar
ria

Serui

S mada
na

sketching.) But there were no computers in 1500: and this ability to organise space into two dimensions, and to turn buildings round in it, may above all have been the special skill that Jacopo alone could have contributed to Kolb's great project. It is little wonder that Dürer, himself one of the greatest of draughtsmen, had so much respect for Jacopo's technical skills.

No less remarkable than the draughtsmanship was the actual printing of the great map. From edge to edge, the impression is crisp and clean, without a trace of ink spread and with hatched shading lines beautifully sharp and clear across the entire surface of the map, though spaced as close as 50 to the inch (20 per cm). It has to be admitted that this is not remarkable by modern standards, and that Dürer's woodcuts were just as well printed: but none of Dürer's work begins to approach the enormous size of Jacopo's woodcuts, and I suspect that few modern printers would volunteer to reach Kolb's standards with wooden blocks, a wooden press and hand inking. By any standards the map is superbly printed: given the technology of AD 1500 it is mind-blowing.

Some kind of printing from wooden blocks had been known since the 1300s, and the earliest dated woodcut was made in 1423. These early prints were made by inking the block with a leather pad, laying upon it the sheet of paper to be printed, and burnishing the back of the sheet by hand. Mainly

TIMELESS VENICE

of religious subjects (the 1423 print is of St Christopher) such prints were limited to a rough picture plus a few words of text. The development of printing had to await two great inventions, both of which are customarily attributed to Johann Gutenberg of Mainz.

Gutenberg started his experiments some time before 1440 and printed his great bible in 1456. The major contributions to printing that are credited to him were the inventions of moveable type and the printing press, which together began the information explosion that has, perhaps more than any other factor, revolutionised human activities in the last five hundred years.

Urged on by the Renaissance thirst for knowledge, the new art of printing grew within a brief lifetime into a major industry, particularly in Venice, where the freethinking atmosphere and virtual absence of ecclesiastical censorship offered the best possible environment for printers. The number of printers' workshops in Venice by 1500 is variously estimated at between 65 and 100. It was here that Aldo Manucci (more grandly known as Aldus Manutius) came in 1490 to print his great editions of the Greek and Latin classics, and we are told that by the end of the 15th century more books had been published in Venice than in Rome, Milan, Florence and Naples put together.

THE ACHIEVEMENT OF JACOPO AND HIS COLLEAGUES

Printing presses at this time were made mostly or entirely of wood, and were usually fixed to the ceiling for stability. 'Considerable muscular effort' is said to have been necessary to operate them. Moran writes: 'The power of the wooden press was limited to the amount of force the platen could exert upon an area of type... when printing more than one page on a sheet of paper became the requirement, the limited power made it necessary to print half a sheet at a time, with two pulls of the bar. The largest wooden press ever built would seem to be that mentioned by John Johnson in *Typographia* (1824) – a double royal size (platen 2 feet 2 inches by 1 foot 8 inches) built for "the old Duke of Norfolk".' The date of the old Duke's wooden press is not clear from this mention of it, but it sounds as though it must have been within living memory in 1824.

It is unlikely that Jacopo's map was printed with 'two pulls of the bar', however. As Moran says, this technique was suitable to the printing of two pages on one sheet: if applied to a single page or a single block, it would have resulted in an obvious break or overlap down the middle. So the old Duke's claim to 'the largest wooden press ever built' would seem to be challenged by the press on which Jacopo's map must have been printed. The Duke's platen size of 26 by 20 inches would not have accommodated even half of one of Jacopo's 40 by 27 inch blocks. One can hardly doubt, then, that Kolb must

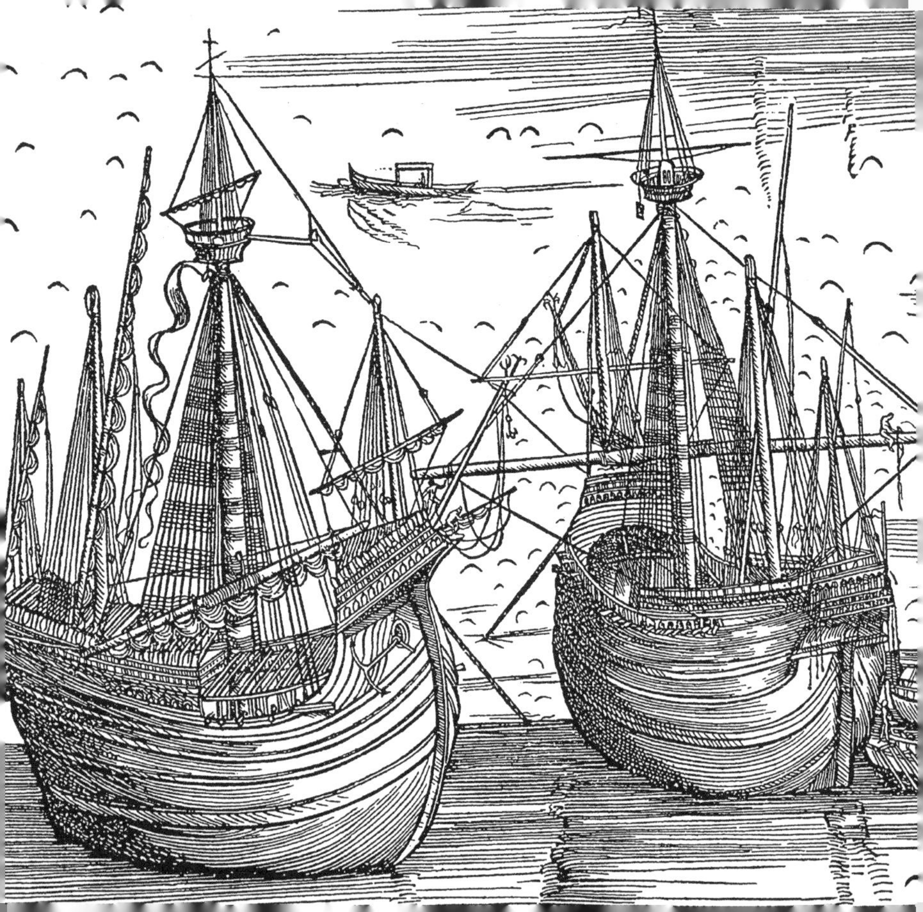

have had an enormous press built for the unique purpose of printing the map, since there appears to be no record of any other formes of such size having been printed at or even near that period.

Such a press would have been too cumbersome for printing anything smaller, so one is forced to conclude that it would have been scrapped as useless after the map ceased to be printed. How else could a monster press capable of dealing with the map have vanished so completely from the history of printing? Balistreri-Trincanato, a modern authority on the map, even postulates six separate presses, one for each block, on the grounds that any press leaves its own 'footprint' on the sheet it prints, and that the six sheets of Jacopo's map all show different footprints. Questioned on the likelihood of six giant presses being made to print one map, he replies that printing in Venice in 1500 was a ferment of new technology, and that nothing can be ruled out as impossible.

The size of the largest paper used by Caxton (in 1483) was 15¾ by 22 inches, according to Hunter. He writes: 'This size was probably found too large for convenient printing, as for all of the other Caxton books smaller paper was used, varying in size from 11 by 16 to 13 by 18½ inches. In Great Britain even as late as 1818 it was ordained by law that no newspaper should exceed in dimensions 22 by 32 inches. About the largest surface of the fifteenth-century papers was 470 square inches. The largest size of handmade paper that is fabricated at present is made in the James Whatman, Springfield mill at Maidstone, Kent, the sheet being termed "antiquarian" and measuring 31 by 53 inches, a surface of 1643 square inches. For making sheets of this giant size the mould is hung on a mechanical lifting device and six or eight men are required in the dipping and couching processes'.

It is true that Kolb's paper is smaller than this present-day 'giant size': but measuring more than 27 by 39 inches, it is well over double the area of Hunter's 'largest' fifteenth-century paper. Indeed Kolb's claim that the map had required sheets of paper larger than any made before, and had demanded the latest techniques of printing large formes, was far from being an overstatement. A modern publisher might consider himself guilty of shameful underselling if, having brought out anything remotely comparable, he failed to describe it at least as a technological miracle.

Epilogue

INEVITABLY in this CD-ROM and in this note I have dealt mainly with physical matters, with buildings and canals, with wood blocks and printing. But for me, Jacopo's map has a deep emotional charge beyond its significance as art or craftsmanship. I have no doubt that Kolb and Jacopo were celebrating a glory that they believed could have no end. In fact they were writing Venice's funeral eulogy.

In 1453 the Turks had taken Constantinople, Venice's power base in the eastern Mediterranean. In 1496 Columbus reached the mainland of America. In 1498 Vasco da Gama rounded the Cape of Good Hope and established the sea route to India. In March 1500 thirteen merchant ships left Lisbon for Calicut. Venice's commercial *raison d'etre* – the mastery of the old trade routes between Europe and the East – evaporated like dew in midsummer as world trade dribbled out of the Mediterranean and into the Atlantic. Henceforward, world sea power would mean not Venice but Holland, Spain and England. Kolb's half-millennium celebration of Venice turned out to be its epitaph. I know of nothing else – not even Pompeii – that conveys so poignantly this frozen final moment of triumph, this last pirouette before the le .

EPILOGUE

banana skin, this instant when, all unknown to its passengers, the rocket stopped going up and the stick started coming down.

Never has there been a greater pride than that of Venice in 1500. Rarely can there have been a greater fall. Yet so great had been the strength, the wealth, the charisma, of this wonderful city that it took another three centuries – and Napoleon Bonaparte – to bring it to its last humiliation of seventy years of French and Austrian military occupation.

Venice never recovered as a political or economic force. Yet it has risen again in a way that would have been perfectly familiar to the tourist-conscious Venetians of 1500 – and to an extent that they could not have foreseen in their wildest imaginings. Its beauty merely enhanced by the patina of time, its ancient magic uncorrupted and incorruptible, Venice has become the dream city of millions of visitors from parts of the world that Jacopo, Kolb, their engravers and their printers never even knew existed.

A few years ago, alone among the graffiti sprayed on the outside wall of the Arsenale, one caught my eye. It was the rallying-cry of the old Venetians, who used to shout the name of their city's patron saint as they went into battle. And while these days it probably has more to do with Venice's football team than with military matters, it seems to me still to express the Venetians' traditional feelings of identity, of pride and of separateness:

Viva Sammarco!

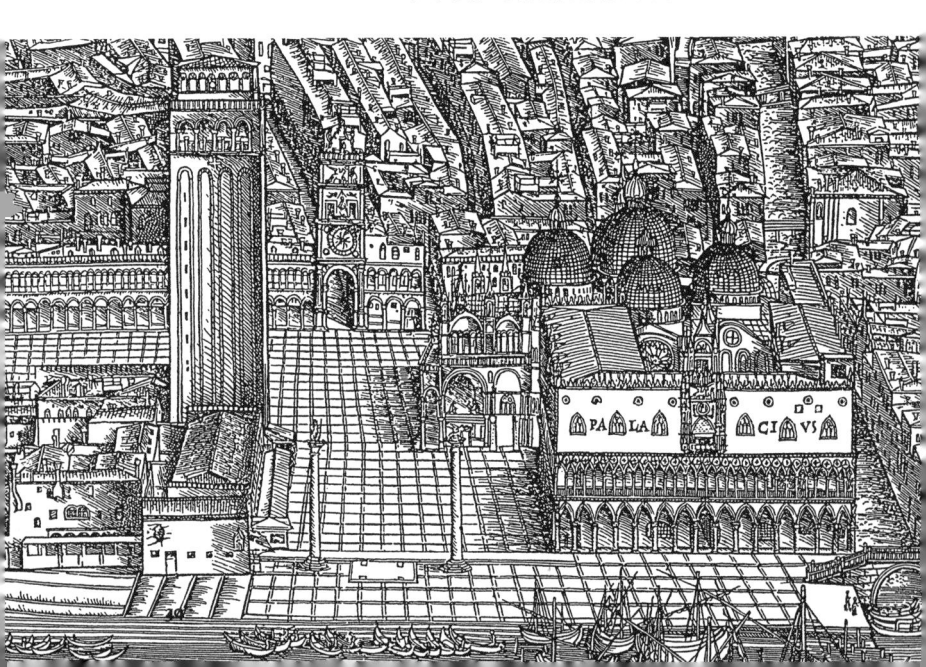

Author's note

Of the dozen or so known original prints of Jacopo's map, every one has suffered some degree of damage in the past five centuries. Most or all have been retouched to a greater or lesser extent. As a result, one cannot say that there is any truly authentic original, though the print in the British Museum is generally agreed to be the best preserved of those existing.

The map has excited the interest of scholars for at least 150 years. But until the advent of modern photography and photocopying, it was hardly possible to appreciate fully its staggering detail. Standing in front of a museum copy, for example, how would one count 253 bridges, 377 oarsmen or 10,357 chimney-pots, as Balistreri-Trincanato and Zanverdiani[1] have done? A major breakthrough came with the publication in 1962, by the Cassa di Risparmio di Venezia (the Venetian Savings Bank), of a full-sized copy of the map in six sheets. Reproduced from the British Museum print, and published in a limited edition, this is now greatly prized and must have been largely responsible for the enormous surge in scholarly articles about the map which have appeared in recent years, especially in Venice.

[1] In their book *Jacopo de Barbari: Il Racconto di una Città*.

Some years later came the publication in Venice of another full-sized copy in six sheets, printed by Foligraf of Mestre. Compiled by the late Ezio Tedeschi from originals in Venice, which contain somewhat more retouching than the British Museum print, it has been criticised as being less than 'authentic' in places. However, such places are few and far between, and its printing is so 'clean' that I had little hesitation in choosing the Tedeschi version as the source of illustrations for this CD-ROM. From the public viewpoint, too, the Tedeschi version has the merit of being on unlimited sale from Signor Tedeschi's son Marco through his company Edizioni Tedeschi Marco, not only as six full-sized sheets for serious study, but also as a single sheet one metre wide which looks very handsome in a frame.

On the point of retouching, I must admit to having added a little of my own in two or three places, where I think it adds to the accuracy of the reproduction without, I hope, being obtrusive. In a very few places, too, the viewer may notice a slight 'saw-tooth' effect where the image is very much enlarged. This is due to the necessary digital scanning of the map for computer reproduction, and to that extent is unfaithful to the original. Once again, I hope that this will not detract from the overall enjoyment of Jacopo's masterpiece.

My reason for making this CD-ROM is simple. When I first fell under the spell of Jacopo's map nearly thirty years ago, I found there was no book that

AUTHOR'S NOTE

would give me basic information about it. Before I could read such a book, I first had to write it. But there are plenty of books about Venice already; and having written my book, I could not find a publisher willing to invest in what appeared to be a highly specialised subject. Indeed, it was only quite recently by chance, in the studio of my designer friend Hilary Sadler, that I saw a CD-ROM for the first time – and realised that here was the perfect medium for my work. After that, it was just a matter of taking three hundred or so colour photographs (my previous ones had been in black-and-white), getting my copy of the map scanned professionally, buying a computer and a copy of Macromedia's Director 7 authoring program and learning how to drive them, and putting it all together.

I would like here to express my gratitude to Ms Karen L Marshall of Save Venice Inc., and to Signor Marco Tedeschi, for each kindly contributing a photograph of theirs where I had none of my own. I thank especially Hilary Sadler, who rescued this project many years ago when it was going through a bad patch, and whose almost invincible good nature has withstood the many alterations and bright ideas I have inflicted on him.

I believe Jacopo's map to be one of the greatest and most fascinating masterworks of all time. I want to share it with as many people as I can.

M.R.

Some Italian and Venetian terms

Ca': Venetian for *casa*, a house. Used in the same way as *palazzo*.

Campanile: Bell tower.

Campo: Square, usually attached to a church (lit. field).

Palazzo: Large house, most often named after a family of present or past owners.

Ponte: Bridge.

Rio: Canal (lit. brook).

Sotoportego: Passage under a house, usually to a central courtyard but sometimes in the form of a walkway beside a canal.

The suffixes *-ello* and *-etto* are sometimes used for a small *campo*, *palazzo* etc., thus: *campiello, palazzetto*.

Locations of original prints of the map

First state:

Berlin: Staatliche Museen

Boston, Mass.: Museum of Fine Arts

Cleveland, Ohio: Museum of Art

Hamburg: Kunsthalle

London: British Museum

Nuremberg: Germanisches National Museum

Paris: Bibliotèque Nationale

Venice: Fondazione Querini Stampalia

Venice: Museo Correr

Later states:

Amsterdam: Rijksprentenkabinet

Austin, Texas: University of Texas

Florence: private collection

London: British Museum

Los Angeles: University of California, Grunwald Graphic Arts Foundation

Venice: Biblioteca Marciana

Venice: Museo Correr

Venice: private collection

Vienna: Albertina

Washington, DC: National Gallery of Art

Main sources consulted for the CD-ROM and this note

In English:

Hunter, D: *Papermaking: the history and technique of an ancient craft*, Alfred A Knopf, New York, 1947.

Lorenzetti G (transl. Guthrie J): *Venice and its lagoon*, Istituto Poligrafico dello Stato, Libreria dello Stato, Rome 1961.

Moran, J: *Printing Presses*, University of California Press, 1973.

Schulz, J: *Jacopo de' Barbari's View of Venice: Map Making, City Views, and Moralized Geography Before the Year 1500*, in *The Art Bulletin*, LX-3, College Art Association of America, New York, 1978.

MAIN SOURCES CONSULTED FOR THE CD-ROM AND THIS NOTE

In Italian:

Pignatti T: *La pianta* in *La pianta prospettica di Venezia del 1500*, Cassa di Risparmio, Venezia, 1962.

Tassini, G: Curiosità Veneziane, (1863), 9th edition, Filippi Editore, Venezia, 1988.

Romanelli G et al: *A volo d'uccello: Jacopo de' Barbari e le rappresentazioni di città nell'Europa del Rinascimento,* Arsenale Editrice, Venezia Mestre, 1999.

Falchetta, P: *Jacopo de Barbari e le vedute di Venezia: una guida multimediale,* http://www.tin.it/veniva/venetie/home.htm, 2000.

Balistreri-Trincanato, C and Zanverdiani, D: *Jacopo de' Barbari: il racconto di una città,* Edizioni Stamperia Cetid, Venezia-Mestre, 2000.

S Luca

How to buy prints of the map

In this CD-ROM, images from Jacopo de' Barbari's map of Venice in 1500 are reproduced by permission from the restored edition published by

Edizioni Tedeschi Marco, Via Fornase 50, 30038 Spinea (Venezia), Italy.

Prints are available in two versions: full size facsimile (six sheets), and reduced size (single sheet, one metre wide). Both are of excellent quality, and show the map in full detail. The reduced size is suitable for framing and is available from the website

www.TimelessVenice.com

For details and price of the full size facsimile version in six sheets, please write to Edizioni Tedeschi Marco.

Please also visit the website *www.TimelessVenice.com* to buy further copies of this CD-ROM and booklet.

Trouble-shooting

This CD-ROM is configured for PCs with speakers and with Pentium 100 or faster, running Windows 95 or later, and for Macs with PowerPC processor using System 7.5 or later. It may not be suitable for use on a network. You should exit all other applications before running it.

If program does not start

PC: When you insert the CD-ROM, the program should start automatically within 30 seconds or so. If it does not, it may mean that your computer is not set up for autorun. In this case, select *Start* followed by *Run*. Type *D:\Start.exe* (where *D* is the name of your CD drive) and press *Enter*.

To set up your computer for autorun, go to *Windows Help*, search for *CDs, automatic* and follow the instructions.

Mac: After inserting the CD, open the folder and double-click the *Start.Mac* icon.

TROUBLE-SHOOTING

No sound when program starts

PC: If your PC starts to show the program, but you get no sound, check the speakers and volume controls. If you still get no sound, your computer may not be set up to play *.WAV* sound files. In this case, go to *Windows Help,* search for *Volume Control,* and follow the steps needed to show the *Wave* volume control. Check that this is not disabled or muted, and that the 'slider' on the screen is near the top of its panel. If necessary, use your mouse to move it upwards.

Mac: Check the output speaker and volume controls in the *Control Panels* folder.

ISBN 1 873429 98 3

© Copyright 2003 Mark Robinson & Hilary Sadler
TimelessVenice.com

VENETIE
MD